Welcome to Monday:

52 Devotionals for the Weekly Struggle

Chad Krahn

Copyright © 2025 Chad Krahn

All rights reserved. No part of this publication may be reproduced, stored in a retrieval system, or transmitted in any form or by any means—electronic, mechanical, photocopying, recording, or otherwise—without the prior written permission of the publisher, except in the case of brief quotations embodied in critical articles or reviews.

ISBN: 978-1-068660061

Printed in Canada
First printed in 2025

Published by Nine Tries LTD
6 Artisans Dwellings
Saffron Walden, Essex
CB10 1LW
United Kingdom

ninetries.co.uk

For Heather, who is always willing to come on the adventure.

And for all those willing to struggle forward to illuminate the darkness.

Blessings.

Introduction

IT ALL BEGAN WITH A SIMPLE IDEA: could a well-timed text message on Monday morning hit as hard as a good sermon? As someone who cares deeply about the spiritual lives of others, especially men, I wanted to offer more than just casual encouragement. I aimed to help equip men for the battles we face against the world, the flesh, and the devil, right at the start of each week.

So, I started sending Monday morning texts to a group of twenty men I cared about. These weren't intended to be long-winded or preachy messages, but short, direct hits—just a few sentences designed to challenge, inspire, or reframe our approach to the coming days. There's something significant about Monday mornings; it's when the weight of the week ahead settles in, and our battles—spiritual and otherwise—begin anew.

One of the first devotionals I sent reflected on C.S. Lewis's words from *Mere Christianity*. Lewis draws a distinction between sins of the flesh and deeper spiritual sins: "The sins of the flesh are bad, but they are the least bad of all sins. All the worst pleasures are purely spiritual... the pleasures of power, of hatred."[1] His wisdom set the tone for this project. While we must fight against the flesh, our subtler and more dangerous battles are often spiritual. This particular message prompted me to reflect deeply on the struggle between our "Animal self" and our "Diabolical self," a theme that resonates throughout this collection.

Another early message explored the idea of duality—not as a cosmic yin and yang, but as a battle between truth and its perversion. Again, I quoted Lewis, this time from *The Great Divorce*: "Heaven is reality itself... all that can be shaken will be shaken and only the

---

1. C.S. Lewis, Mere Christianity (New York: HarperCollins, 2001), 95–96.

unshakeable remains."[2] These words reminded both me and the men receiving these texts that we aren't caught in an eternal balance between good and evil. Instead, we stand firmly on the side of truth, resisting distortions of that truth.

As these Monday messages continued, they became a weekly rhythm—for me as the writer and for those who received them. Some devotionals were brief, perhaps too brief to fully capture the broader themes I wanted to explore. This realization led me here, to this collection. What began as quick-fire texts evolved into fuller, more substantial devotionals—messages that dig deeper into our struggles against temptation, sin, and the subtle lies of the enemy.

This book isn't merely about Monday mornings; it addresses the battles we fight every day. It's not just for men either, because the biblical wisdom is universal. It calls us beyond passivity and spiritual laziness toward action—sometimes through small steps, sometimes through leaps of faith—as we mature into the people God has called us to become. My hope is that these devotionals will be tools in your hands, just as those Monday texts were intended—a well-timed hit to get you back in the fight, ready for the week ahead.

Grace be with you; we have much darkness to illuminate.

—Chad

---

2. C.S. Lewis, The Great Divorce (New York: HarperOne, 2001), 72.

1. Jesus Is King

WELCOME TO MONDAY. Our battle against the world, the flesh, and the devil continues.

When we sing about Jesus as "the King" or "our King," it's easy to let those words slip by without truly grasping their significance. This phrase is more than just a title; it is a declaration of war against the very forces that seek to enslave us. In John 12:31, Jesus refers to Satan as the ruler, or prince, of this world. If Satan holds sway over the world—whether partially or fully—it explains the pervasive suffering, deception, and pain we witness daily.

In a monarchy, the end of a ruling dynasty comes only through conflict. When we declare Jesus as our King through our words and actions, we essentially declare war on Satan's reign, challenging his legitimacy. This is not a call to arms in the physical sense but rather a spiritual battle fought through prayer, faith, and devotion. I've seen this in my own life—times when it would have been easy to let despair creep in, choosing to pray and choosing to do the right things felt like taking a stand in the middle of a wave of chaos. Colossians 2:15 declares, "He disarmed the rulers and authorities and put them to open shame, by triumphing over them in him." This assures us that Christ's kingship has already defeated the enemy, empowering us to stand firm.

Today, let us envision the new kingdom that Jesus will bring. We are called to be agents of that kingdom here and now, illuminating the darkness around us with the light of Christ. Every act of obedience—whether forgiving a coworker or serving a neighbor—proclaims Jesus' reign and pushes back the enemy's influence.

Grace be with you; we have much darkness to illuminate.

Further Reading

John 12:31–32

"Now is the judgment of this world; now will the ruler of this world be cast out. And I, when I am lifted up from the earth, will draw all people to myself."

Application

This week, consider how your actions declare who is truly King in your life. Are you living as a citizen of Jesus' kingdom, or are you allowing the world to dictate your priorities? Take time to reflect on one way you can submit more fully to His reign—whether in prayer, a decision, or an act of service. Set a daily reminder to pray: "Jesus, You are my King; guide my steps." Journal one moment each day where you chose Christ's authority over worldly pressures. For example, if you're tempted to argue, choose peace instead and note how it reflects Jesus' reign. By week's end, review how these choices strengthened your faith.

2. The Enemy's Plans

WELCOME TO MONDAY. Our battle against the world, the flesh, and the devil continues.

Remember, Satan hates you and has a terrible plan for your life. Perhaps not the encouragement you were hoping for this morning! Yet, as you navigate your day, ask yourself: how might my actions in this situation align with or resist the enemy's intentions?

Take a moment today to meditate on Ephesians 6:10–18. Too often, we confine the "armor of God" passage to Vacation Bible School lessons or charismatic circles. However, these verses represent powerful ancient Near Eastern imagery. The early church saw them as essential for believers to internalize, recognizing their practical value in our daily spiritual battles.

Grace be with you; we have much darkness to illuminate.

Further Reading

Ephesians 6:11–17

"Put on the whole armor of God, that you may be able to stand against the schemes of the devil. For we do not wrestle against flesh and blood, but against the rulers, against the authorities, against the cosmic powers over this present darkness, against the spiritual forces of evil in the heavenly places. Therefore take up the whole armor of God, that you may be able to withstand in the evil day, and having done all, to stand firm. Stand therefore, having fastened on the belt of truth, and having put on the breastplate of righteousness, and, as shoes for your feet, having put on the readiness given by the gospel of peace.In all circumstances take up the shield of faith, with which you can extinguish all the flaming darts of the evil one; and take the helmet of salvation, and the sword of the Spirit, which is the word of God."

Application

This week, acknowledge the reality of spiritual opposition without succumbing to fear. Instead, live with preparedness. Reflect honestly: how might the enemy attempt to derail me this week? Identify your vulnerabilities, and deliberately put on the armor of God—truth, righteousness, faith, salvation, and the Word—so you can stand firm. (Ephesians 6:10–18)

Prayerfully affirm your readiness each day: "Lord, help me put on Your armor and walk faithfully."

3. BATTLE AGAINST LIES

WELCOME TO MONDAY. Our battle with the world, the flesh, and the devil continues.

We live in a world saturated with lies. Advertising has evolved from merely persuading us to buy a product to compelling us toward deeper desires, influencing our sense of identity and purpose. This struggle isn't simply about temptation for superficial indulgences; it touches the deeper wiring of our flesh, pulling us toward excess, indifference, and ultimately, self-destruction.

Remember, the devil—the father of lies—works more subtly than we often realize. C.S. Lewis illustrates this vividly in *The Screwtape Letters* when Screwtape, an elder demon, commented to his understudy: "It is funny how mortals always picture us as putting things into their minds: in reality, our best work is done by keeping things out."[1] The enemy's strategy is seldom blatant temptation but rather subtle deception, twisting truth until we hardly recognize reality.

Today, let's acknowledge the battle we're in and consciously reject lies. Let us renew our minds in truth, as Romans 12:2 instructs us, transforming our lives rather than conforming to the world's deceit.

Grace be with you; we have much darkness to illuminate.

Further Reading

Romans 12:2

"Do not be conformed to this world, but be transformed by the renewal of your mind, that by testing you may discern what is the will of God, what is good and acceptable and perfect."

---

[1]. C.S. Lewis, *The Screwtape Letters* (New York: Macmillan, 1961).

Application

This week, examine the lies you encounter in daily life. Reflect honestly: Which subtle lies influence your choices and identity? Intentionally counteract these lies by aligning your thoughts and actions with God's truth. Spend time renewing your mind through Scripture, discerning clearly what is good, acceptable, and perfect.

4. The Original Lie

Welcome to Monday. Our battle against the world, the flesh, and the devil continues.

The original lie the devil used was, "Did God really say...?" In hindsight, the deception seems obvious (yes, He certainly did say that!), yet the lie remains subtle, quietly casting doubt on truths we already know. This uncertainty can be brushed aside by the rhetorical reminder: "If you have to ask the question..."

At some point this week, the phrase "Did God really say...?" will slip into your mind. Guaranteed. It might manifest as a thought like, "Is it really that bad?", "You couldn't possibly need to...", or "I'm sure no one would mind."

Your mission this week is to anticipate that moment. Equip yourself with truth to counter those subtle doubts. Remember: the enemy's strategy is to sow uncertainty, but faith can uproot these doubts before they take hold.

Grace be with you; we have much darkness to illuminate.

Further Reading

Genesis 3:1-4

"Now the serpent was more crafty than any other beast of the field that the Lord God had made. He said to the woman, 'Did God actually say, "You shall not eat of any tree in the garden"?' The woman said to the serpent, "We may eat the fruit of the trees of the garden, but concerning the fruit of the tree in the midst of the garden, God said, 'You shall not eat it, nor shall you touch it, lest you die.'"

Application

Be alert this week for the whisper, "Did God really say...?". When you hear it, stop immediately and counter it with truth. Regularly meditate on Scripture so that when doubt arises, you respond with clarity and conviction.

5. Fear Not!

Welcome to Monday. Our battle against the world, the flesh, and the devil continues.

Fear motivates much of what we do—or feel compelled to do. From the fear of missing out, to impostor syndrome, to disappointing others, fear becomes a constant force behind our decisions. Our animal brain (the flesh) is hardwired to respond instinctively to fear, often pushing us toward self-preservation or hasty choices. People spend their lives driven by fears they rarely acknowledge—worries about illness, anxiety over societal collapse, or dread of an uncertain future. This quickly becomes a trap, causing us to forget Jesus's clear command: "Fear not!"

Yoda once warned, "Fear is the path to the dark side. Fear leads to anger. Anger leads to hate. Hate leads to suffering." This isn't just pop culture wisdom; it reflects a spiritual truth. Fear can ensnare us, nudging us toward harmful shortcuts or paralyzing inaction. Consider the Israelites at the edge of the Promised Land (Numbers 13–14). Sent to scout Canaan, ten of the twelve spies returned gripped by fear, describing giants and fortified cities. Their fear spread like a contagion, leading the people to rebel against God's promise. Only Joshua and Caleb, anchored in faith, urged trust in God's abundance. Fear distorted reality, turning a land of milk and honey into a death trap in their minds.

The enemy loves to amplify fear, whispering that we're too weak or the stakes are too high. But Jesus's command to "fear not" isn't a suggestion—it's a call to reorient our perspective. Isaiah 41:10 reminds us that God is with us, strengthening and upholding us. This week, pay attention to your motivations. Are your actions driven by fear or guided by faith? When fear creeps in, pause and recall a moment when God proved faithful in your life—perhaps an answered prayer or an unexpected provision. Let that memory anchor you, reminding you that the God who delivered you then is with you now.

Grace be with you; we have much darkness to illuminate.

Further Reading

Isaiah 41:10

"Fear not, for I am with you; be not dismayed, for I am your God; I will strengthen you, I will help you, I will uphold you with my righteous right hand."

Application

Fear creeps in unnoticed, often masquerading as caution or pragmatism. This week, whenever you sense worry or fear rising, use it as a trigger for prayer. Speak God's truth over your fear, whether through Scripture, worship, or simply declaring: "I will not fear, for God is with me." Keep a small notebook or note on your phone to jot down moments when fear tempts you. Beside each, write a truth from Scripture (e.g., "God is my strength" from Isaiah 41:10). At the end of the week, review your notes to see how God met you in those moments. Intentionally replace fear with faith by taking one bold step—perhaps initiating a difficult conversation or trusting God with a decision you've been avoiding.

6. Apathy

WELCOME TO MONDAY. Our battle against the world, the flesh, and the devil continues.

This week, our spiritual enemies will do their utmost to grind you into both apathy and entropy. You may be tempted to think, "Things will always get worse. The world is falling apart. Nothing will ever improve." Bart Simpson's famous quip, "Can't win. Don't try," might linger at the edge of your mind.

While it may be true that things could get worse, that very reality calls for engagement rather than withdrawal. In the midst of struggle, Jesus taught us to pray, "Your kingdom come, on earth as it is in heaven."

Recently, I've found it helpful to make this prayer personal and local by adding the city where I live into the words of the Lord's Prayer. Now, I say, "...in Red Deer as it is in heaven." I'd recommend that you do the same, substituting in wherever you live. After all, we have much to pray for, and engaging earnestly in prayer can spark meaningful change in our community and beyond.

Grace be with you; we have much darkness to illuminate.

Further Reading

Matthew 6:9-13

"Pray then like this: 'Our Father in heaven, hallowed be your name. Your kingdom come, your will be done, in [your city] as it is in heaven. Give us this day our daily bread, and forgive us our debts, as we also have forgiven our debtors. And lead us not into temptation, but deliver us from evil.'"

Application

This week, take one concrete action to counter spiritual apathy. Pray intentionally for your city, engage in a spiritual discipline you've neglected, or actively encourage someone else's faith. Do something deliberate that moves you beyond passivity.

7. Be On Guard

Welcome to Monday. Our battle against the world, the flesh, and the devil continues.

This week, stay alert against exhaustion and overconfidence. It's tempting to lower our defences, expecting just another ordinary week. Yet, beware—these coming days have the potential to set the tone for the year ahead. The enemy loves exploiting weariness and a false sense of security, leaving us vulnerable to discouragement and distraction.

Remember, we're not pressing forward by our own strength alone. God Himself fights with us and for us. In moments of overwhelm or complacency, hold onto the promise from Philippians: "May the peace of God, which surpasses all understanding, guard your hearts and minds in Christ Jesus." This peace isn't merely an emotion; it's God's own presence fortifying our faith, providing a refuge amid chaos.

Take time this week to reflect: What does it mean to guard your heart and mind? Which thoughts are taking root—are they aligned with God's truth? As you face challenges, ask the Lord to anchor you in His peace, steadying you through every storm.

Grace be with you; we have much darkness to illuminate.

Further Reading

Philippians 4:6–7

"Do not be anxious about anything, but in every situation, by prayer and petition, with thanksgiving, present your requests to God. And the peace of God, which transcends all understanding, will guard your hearts and your minds in Christ Jesus."

Application

Set a daily reminder on your phone this week for a quick check-in: Am I feeling weary or overly confident? Pray intentionally for God's peace to guard your heart and mind.

8. Waiting For The Whisper

WELCOME TO MONDAY. Our battle against the world, the flesh, and the devil continues.

Today, I'm reflecting on the powerful story from 1 Kings 19, where Elijah waits for God's voice. Standing on the mountain, Elijah witnessed a mighty wind tearing mountains apart, but God wasn't in the wind. Then came an earthquake, but God wasn't in the earthquake either. Afterward, a fierce fire blazed, but again, God wasn't in the fire. Finally, God spoke to Elijah in a gentle whisper.

How often do we become caught up in life's chaos, anxiously seeking God's guidance? We recall past storms, often retroactively deciding what God taught us through them—but did we ever pause to wait patiently for His quiet voice? The world pushes us forward relentlessly, rarely giving space to hear that whisper.

Inevitably, some unwelcome chaos will erupt this week. Amidst potential panic and confusion, pause and wait for the whisper. It's often in the stillness that God reveals Himself.

Grace be with you; we have much darkness to illuminate.

Further Reading

1 Kings 19:11–12

"And he said, 'Go out and stand on the mount before the Lord.' And behold, the Lord passed by, and a great and strong wind tore the mountains and broke in pieces the rocks before the Lord, but the Lord was not in the wind. And after the wind an earthquake, but the Lord was not in the earthquake. And after the earthquake a fire, but the Lord was not in the fire. And after the fire the sound of a low whisper."

Application

Carve out intentional silence this week—morning, commute, or evening (but not in bed)—to quietly wait and listen for God's whisper. Silence distractions and simply be present with Him. This will likely be harder than you think, but it's critical to do.

9. Intentional Growth

Welcome to Monday. Our battle against the world, the flesh, and the devil continues.

We often wish life would happen organically—that everything meaningful would naturally fall into place. Yet experience teaches us otherwise: anything valuable demands time, effort, and intentionality. Meaningful relationships and spiritual depth require focused commitment. When we say we want things to happen "organically," we often mean we prefer them to happen effortlessly or by chance. However, just like organic farming, which is a more intentional and labor-intensive process than non-organic methods, meaningful growth in our spiritual lives cannot happen by drifting along, hoping for improvement.

Our prayer lives require this same level of deliberate effort, if not more, because neglect comes easily. This week, consider practising fixed-hour prayer, an ancient tradition observed by monasteries that pause at scheduled times throughout the day. Set your phone alarm at three points during the day—morning, afternoon, and evening—and slowly, intentionally pray the Lord's Prayer. Personally, I've found 9:38 am, 1:33 pm, and 10:00 pm effective moments to refocus, pausing intentionally. Whenever possible, when the alarm goes off, physically move to another room, kneel, and pray. These moments puncture our routines, reminding us of the Lord's presence and goodness.

Grace be with you; we have much darkness to illuminate.

Further Reading

1 Corinthians 9:24–27

"Do you not know that in a race all the runners run, but only one receives the prize? So run that you may obtain it. Every athlete exercises self-control in all things. They do it to receive a perishable wreath, but we an imperishable. So I do not run aimlessly; I do not box as one beating the air. But I discipline my body and keep it under control, lest after preaching to others I myself should be disqualified."

Application

Practice fixed-hour prayer this week. Set alarms at three distinct times each day—morning, afternoon, and evening. Slowly recite the Lord's Prayer, then pause briefly in silence, welcoming God's presence.

10. The Battle of Comfort vs. Discipline

Welcome to Monday. Our battle against the world, the flesh, and the devil continues.

Remember that your flesh conspires against you. Our world is designed to cater to your comfort and ease. It's easy to pour one more drink, keep scrolling through social media, or let Netflix autoplay another episode. Quiet lies creep in, telling you that you deserve it, that you've earned this indulgence.

On the other hand, setting aside time for prayer is challenging. It's difficult to sit in silence before God, to fast, or give generously to those in need. Spiritual disciplines demand focused effort because the same subtle voice encouraging indulgence whispers that discipline isn't worth it. So, ask yourself: do you want to live life in easy mode or hard mode? Choose wisely—it's a life-or-death choice.

Isn't it ironic that we seek comfort in watching people far more disciplined than ourselves? I watch a lot of Oilers games, and I'm fairly certain Connor McDavid is one of the most disciplined people ever, obviously never skipping leg day. His relentless training and drive is a big part of what makes him a great player. Yet, I'm willing to sit around burning time on social media rather than communing with the creator. We feel guilt when we skip a gym session, but do we feel the same about missing prayer or neglecting a neighbor in need? Skipping spiritual workouts risks our soul's strength.

Paul's life shows what prioritizing spiritual workouts achieves. In 2 Timothy 4:7–8, he writes, "I have fought the good fight, I have finished the race, I have kept the faith." His discipline won an eternal crown. This week, reject the lure of comfort for the strength of discipline. Each choice to prioritize prayer, generosity, or silence over indulgence builds resilience against the flesh's pull. You're not alone—God's Spirit empowers you to choose the hard but life-giving path.

Grace be with you; we have much darkness to illuminate.

Further Reading

Galatians 5:16–17

"But I say, walk by the Spirit, and you will not gratify the desires of the flesh. For the desires of the flesh are against the Spirit, and the desires of the Spirit are against the flesh, for these are opposed to each other, to keep you from doing the things you want to do."

Application

Choose one small but meaningful discipline to adopt this week. Whether waking earlier to pray, abstaining from distractions, or prioritizing scripture, take one intentional step toward spiritual strength. Journal each evening: note when you chose discipline over comfort and how it shaped your day. Reflect on the irony—when tempted to watch super disciplined people like McDavid, ask, "Why not live with their resolve?" If you feel guilt for skipping a workout, let it prompt conviction for skipping spiritual workouts. If temptation to indulge arises, pray, "Lord, strengthen me to choose Your way." Share your goal with a trusted friend for accountability, checking in midweek. By week's end, reflect on how these choices deepened your faith and purpose.

11. Chop Wood Before Dark

Welcome to Monday. Our battle against the world, the flesh, and the devil continues.

Everyone loves a campfire. In today's world, it's a luxury, but consider how crucial a fire was to ancient travelers. The safety and security it offered against the darkness was invaluable. Yet fires require wood, and gathering it demands effort. It's a relief to arrive at a campsite and find wood already stacked rather than scrambling in the dark. Our spiritual lives mirror this truth—night will inevitably come. Dark times may be less predictable than physical darkness, but they are certain to arrive. Chopping spiritual wood—prayer, fasting, silence, time in Scripture—during daylight builds a reserve for the dark. Many of us run nearly empty, scrambling when darkness descends because we neglected to gather our firewood earlier.

I learned this lesson during a particularly chaotic season for our family. I had some career setbacks and we had a busy house with lots on the go. I hadn't prioritized prayer or Scripture, assuming I could "get by." When a crisis hit—emergency brain surgery for one of our kids—I felt unprepared, grasping for faith in the dark. It was only by returning to simple disciplines, even small ones like a five-minute prayer and reflection, that I began to rebuild my spiritual reserves. I should add that our community supported our family immensely in that season as well; it felt like we borrowed other people's spiritual firewood in that season. The Bible echoes this in Matthew 7:24–25, where Jesus compares the wise man to one who builds on rock before the storm. Preparation matters.

The enemy wants us reactive, not proactive, in our faith. He thrives when we're caught off guard, too weary to fight. But God calls us to diligence now, so we're ready when trials come. This week, identify one spiritual practice to strengthen your reserves. Think of it as chopping wood—each prayer, each verse, each moment of silence stacks your pile higher, preparing you to shine light when darkness falls.

Grace be with you; we have much darkness to illuminate.

Further Reading

Matthew 7:24–25

"Everyone then who hears these words of mine and does them will be like a wise man who built his house on the rock. And the rain fell, and the floods came, and the winds blew and beat on that house, but it did not fall, because it had been founded on the rock."

Application

What spiritual "firewood" do you need before the next storm? Identify one practice—prayer, Scripture reading, or fasting—to strengthen now before a crisis hits. Commit to a specific time each day this week to engage in this discipline, even if it's just 10 minutes. To make it tangible, create a "spiritual woodpile" tracker: draw a stack of logs on a piece of paper and add one log each time you complete your chosen practice. By week's end, reflect on how this habit has fortified you. Pray: "Lord, help me prepare now so I can stand firm in the dark." When challenges arise, remind yourself that every small act of preparation equips you for the battles ahead.

12. Persevering in Practice

Welcome to Monday. Our battle against the world, the flesh, and the devil continues.

I've been reflecting on a quote from Brother Lawrence, a 17th-century French monk known for his humble kitchen tasks, despite being rather clumsy at them. Yet Brother Lawrence mastered the art of practising God's presence in everyday chores. He said, "All things are possible to him who believes, less difficult to him who hopes, easier to him who loves, and still easier to him who practices and perseveres in these three virtues."[1]

This wisdom speaks clearly to us today. Wherever we find ourselves—in menial tasks, routine work, or difficult seasons—persevering in faith, hope, and love bears fruit. Practising these virtues may initially feel difficult, but continued effort makes the burden lighter.

Let this week be marked by your commitment to practising God's presence in all things. Keep pressing forward in belief, hope, and love, even in the smallest tasks. If we seek God there, He will meet us, and perseverance will shape us into who we are meant to be.

Grace be with you; we have much darkness to illuminate.

Further Reading

1 Corinthians 13:13

"So now faith, hope, and love abide, these three; but the greatest of these is love."

---

[1]. Brother Lawrence, *The Practice of the Presence of God*, trans. John Delaney (New York: Image Books, 1977), 55.

Application

Commit to practising God's presence daily. Whether washing dishes, driving, or working, transform these moments into acts of worship by acknowledging God's nearness.

Washing dishes: "Lord, as I clean these dishes, cleanse my heart and renew my spirit."

Doing laundry: "Father, as I wash these clothes, remind me You have made me clean."

Use everyday tasks to remember God is present in every ordinary moment.

13. Renewal

Welcome to Monday. Our battle against the world, the flesh, and the devil continues.

By this time of year, many have forgotten their resolutions—if they even made them. And if you didn't, you might smugly smile as you pass an empty gym. Yet truthfully, opportunities for "newness" constantly appear—new weeks, new months, new seasons. Some feel arbitrary; others are deeply woven into our lives. Ultimately, we all long for renewal—in ourselves and in the world. The enemy, however, wants us stuck, believing change is impossible or reserved for special moments like January 1st.

I didn't set a New Year's resolution, but I chose a word for this year: renewal. I'm thankful for opportunities to reset and start fresh, even during tough times. One practice that anchors me is a breath prayer: "Holy Spirit" (inhale), "Breath of the Living God" (exhale), "Renew me" (inhale), "and all the world" (exhale). I learned this during a season of burnout, when ministry and family life left me depleted. Sitting quietly, breathing this prayer, I felt God's presence restore my weary soul. It's a reminder that renewal isn't a one-time event but a daily invitation. Revelation 21:5 declares, "Behold, I am making all things new." God's work of renewal is ongoing, and we're invited to participate.

The world pulls us toward stagnation, tempting us to coast through life. But God offers a different path—one of continual transformation. This week, embrace the small moments of renewal. A Monday morning, a quiet commute, or a fresh page in your journal can be a sacred space where God makes you new. Pray the breath prayer slowly, and let it reorient your heart toward His renewing work.

Grace be with you; we have much darkness to illuminate.

Further Reading

Revelation 21:5

"And he who was seated on the throne said, 'Behold, I am making all things new.' Also he said, 'Write this down, for these words are trustworthy and true.'"

Application

Pause daily this week to pray this breath prayer: Holy Spirit (inhale)… Breath of the Living God (exhale)… Renew me (inhale)… and all the world (exhale). Allow it to reorient your heart toward renewal. To deepen this practice, set aside five minutes each morning to journal one area of your life where you seek renewal—perhaps a relationship, a habit, or your faith. Write a short prayer asking God to make it new. At the end of the week, review your entries and note any shifts in perspective or peace. When you feel stuck, remind yourself that God's renewal is constant. Pray: "Lord, make me new today, even in the smallest ways." Let each Monday be a fresh start to embrace His transformative work.

14. Silence

WELCOME TO MONDAY. Our battle against the world, the flesh, and the devil continues.

When you woke this morning, it was likely to noise—an alarm clock or a child crying. Our days seem filled with distractions, leaving little space for quiet reflection. Indeed, the elder demon Screwtape confirms that Hell's aim is to saturate the world with noise: "Noise, the grand dynamism, the audible expression of all that is exultant, ruthless, and virile... We will make the whole universe a noise in the end."[1]

Before this sounds merely like an old man longing for quiet, consider how dramatically distractions have increased in recent decades. The world has normalised constant noise, diminishing our ability to escape.

On most days, a moment eventually arrives when the children are in bed and the house grows quiet. Yet even then, we habitually fill the silence with content. Our phones ensure we never experience boredom, and our minds leap to the next worry. Inner quiet seems a luxury reserved only for spiritual gurus.

Yet Jesus regularly sought silence and solitude, connecting deeply with the Father to gain strength, clarity, and peace. Silence is not empty—it's filled with God's presence. Today, we struggle to even go to the bathroom without checking our phones. Reclaiming the ancient discipline of silence before the Lord requires effort, but without it, we risk missing His still, small voice.

Grace be with you; we have much darkness to illuminate.

---

1. C.S. Lewis, The Screwtape Letters (New York: Macmillan, 1961), 91.

Further Reading

Psalm 62:1

"For God alone my soul waits in silence; from him comes my salvation."

Application

This week, set aside intentional time for silence before the Lord. Jesus often chose mornings, but find the best time for you—personally, evenings work well for me.

Begin with a prayer like the Lord's Prayer to centre your mind. Then sit in silence, free from distractions and your phone. Allow your internal chatter to quiet naturally—don't force it. After a few minutes, reflect quietly on God's glory.

Start small—just 5 or 10 minutes each day… and don't check your phone in the bathroom either.

15. The Lie of Entitlement

Welcome to Monday. Our battle against the world, the flesh, and the devil continues.

This week, watch for the subtle lie, "But I deserve this," sneaking into your thoughts. After hard days, long days, or even dull days, entitlement easily creeps in, justifying inaction, indulgence, or even sin. Stay alert—now isn't the time to retreat into obscurity but to press forward into God's call. The world feeds this lie, telling us we're owed comfort, recognition, or reward. But entitlement is a trap, shifting our focus from God's purposes to our own desires.

Whenever the Lord reveals His glory in Scripture, the response is profound humility—a sense of unworthiness. Isaiah, upon seeing God's throne, cried, "Woe is me! For I am lost" (Isaiah 6:5). In that moment, entitlement vanishes. If God clearly commanded something while in His glorious presence, we would act instantly. Yet on this side of glory, we hesitate, justify, and delay, forgetting that "at His right hand are pleasures forevermore" (Psalm 16:11). I recall a time when I felt entitled to a break after a grueling week of work and parenting. I snapped at my kids because I couldn't find the remote while they were going to bed. But that indulgence only left me emptier, and feeling like a lousy parent. It was the gut check of rewatching how I acted in my entitlement that reset my evening.

The enemy uses entitlement to make us self-focused, but God calls us to humility and action. True fulfillment comes not through indulgence but through embracing the good works He has prepared. Life isn't about what we deserve; it's about what He calls us toward. This week, when entitlement whispers, counter it with gratitude and service, remembering that every good thing is a gift of grace.

Grace be with you; we have much darkness to illuminate.

Further Reading

Ephesians 2:10

"For we are his workmanship, created in Christ Jesus for good works, which God prepared beforehand, that we should walk in them."

Application

Whenever you think, "I deserve this," pause and ask, "What is God calling me to in this moment?" Shift from entitlement to gratitude and action. Instead of indulgence, practice generosity—offer time, encouragement, or resources to someone in need. When frustration arises, actively practice thankfulness: name three blessings you've received purely by grace. Each day, pray, "Lord, help me desire what You have for me, not merely what I think I deserve." To make this practical, set a daily alarm for a "gratitude check." When it goes off, write or say one thing you're thankful for and one way you can serve someone else that day. This small habit can rewire your heart, dismantling the lie of entitlement.

16. Judged and Watched

Welcome to Monday. Our battle against the world, the flesh, and the devil continues.

What if you were aware each day of being judged, watched, and evaluated by the spiritual world? We instinctively resist this thought, quickly retreating to comfort ourselves with, "Yes, but I'm forgiven!" While we are indeed forgiven through Christ, this attitude sometimes suggests cheap grace—grace without responsibility or transformation.

Dark forces are ever-present, waiting for opportunities to push you toward spiritual ruin. At the same moment, heavenly forces watch eagerly, hopeful you will become the next vessel through whom God establishes His kingdom more deeply. The spiritual world is far from indifferent to your choices—you participate in a cosmic struggle between good and evil, and your decisions carry eternal significance.

Live as though your life matters profoundly—because it does. Every decision, battle, and victory has meaning on earth and in the unseen realm. Fight with the awareness that your life isn't merely private but a public testimony of faith, grace, and the transformative power of God at work within you.

Grace be with you; we have much darkness to illuminate.

Further Reading

2 Corinthians 5:10

"For we must all appear before the judgment seat of Christ, so that each one may receive what is due for what he has done in the body, whether good or evil."

Application

Live this week mindful that your life is observed—not merely by people, but by heaven itself. When faced with a decision, ask yourself: If this moment were watched on a big screen before all of heaven, how would I act? Let this awareness inspire integrity and faithfulness.

Daily pray: "Lord, help me live today as a testimony of Your grace and truth."

17. THE DUEL OF WILLS

WELCOME TO MONDAY. Our battle against the world, the flesh, and the devil continues.

If you have a strong-willed child, you know exactly what you're in for during confrontations. Perhaps you yourself were that strong-willed child, or maybe your spouse was. These battles can be intense, and the spiritual life often resembles such a struggle—a duel of wills.

In any situation, you'll notice competing wills within you. Your flesh, with its sinful nature, constantly pulls you toward the easy yet wrong path, while your spirit strives for goodness. We often admire individuals who seem exceptionally disciplined, as though they consistently overcome these inner battles. Yet, each of us faces the same struggle daily.

Remember, none of us fight this battle alone. By God's grace and strength, we can choose what is good and persevere.

Grace be with you; we have much darkness to illuminate.

Further Reading

Galatians 5:16-17

"But I say, walk by the Spirit, and you will not gratify the desires of the flesh. For the desires of the flesh are against the Spirit, and the desires of the Spirit are against the flesh, for these are opposed to each other, to keep you from doing the things you want to do."

Application

This week, pay attention to your internal struggle between what is easy and what is right. When drawn to comfort, distraction, or sin, pause and ask, "Which will am I feeding right now—my flesh or my spirit?" Choose the more challenging yet rewarding path, trusting God's strength. Pray: "Lord, help me surrender my will to Yours and walk in Your strength."

18. An Active Prayer for God's Will

Welcome to Monday. Our battle against the world, the flesh, and the devil continues.

There's always a duel of wills—not only within ourselves, between our better nature and sinful flesh, but also throughout life. Whether managing a strong-willed child, handling differing desires in marriage, or even observing the competitive "will to win" in sports, life is full of competing wills. On a cosmic level, the devil seeks to impose his will upon this world.

This leads us to God's will. Modern Christians often pray passively for God's will, offering a list of requests before adding, "But Your will be done, Lord," almost as a way to hedge our prayers.

Yet, Jesus instructs us to actively pray, "Your kingdom come, Your will be done." This isn't passive—it calls for divine action in daily struggles. What if praying for God's will meant inviting His divine power into our everyday lives? We need God's active intervention in our battles.

Grace be with you; we have much darkness to illuminate.

Further Reading

1 Peter 5:6-7

"Humble yourselves, therefore, under the mighty hand of God so that at the proper time he may exalt you, casting all your anxieties on him, because he cares for you."

Application

This week, don't merely pray for God's will—actively step into it. When you say, "Your will be done," ask yourself, "What practical step aligns with my prayer?" Whether reaching out to someone in need, speaking truth, or making a challenging but righteous choice, actively participate in God's work. Pray: "Lord, let Your will be done in my life—not just in words, but in actions."

19. Formed or Deformed

Welcome to Monday. Our battle against the world, the flesh, and the devil continues.

Today, your actions will either form you into Christ's image or you'll be deformed into a sad sack of goo. Life presents us with constant opportunities for growth in holiness or, if we're not careful, for slipping into spiritual stagnation or worse—corruption.

This week, your choices will either guide you toward partaking in the divine nature or allow you to succumb to corruption and the chaos that surrounds us. Every decision matters, from minor daily interactions to significant life choices. We might not always grasp the full weight of our choices in the moment, but each decision shapes us—into Christ's image or into something less.

This is a serious calling, but God's grace equips us to choose wisely. Embrace His divine strength today and walk the path He sets before you.

Grace be with you; we have much darkness to illuminate.

Further Reading

2 Peter 1:3-4

"His divine power has granted to us all things that pertain to life and godliness...that through them you may become partakers of the divine nature, having escaped from the corruption that is in the world because of sinful desire."

Application

This week, intentionally consider what shapes you. Before engaging with any media or people, ask: "Does this form me into Christ's image or deform me into something less?" Place this reminder visibly to prompt reflection. Fill your mind with truth, your words with grace, and your actions with purpose. Pray: "Lord, shape me by Your Word, not by the world."

20. Spiritual Growth in the Struggle

Welcome to Monday. Our battle against the world, the flesh, and the devil continues.

We often experience our greatest spiritual struggles right before significant spiritual breakthroughs. Yet, when we stumble, we wrongly assume our spiritual progress resets. Remember, spiritual setbacks aren't endpoints—they're opportunities for profound growth. The devil is content if we get stuck in one of three modes: prideful in our success, lazy in our spiritual life, or drowning in our failures. However, a repentant believer who continues striving terrifies him. That Christian advances to new spiritual heights, becoming dangerous to darkness precisely because they never quit.

Consider Peter's story in the Gospels. He boldly declared he'd die for Jesus, only to deny Him three times (Luke 22:54–62). That failure could have defined him, but Peter's repentance and Jesus's restoration (John 21:15–19) transformed him into a pillar of the early church. His struggle wasn't a dead end; it was a crucible for growth. This is also true in friendships; many of my best friends are ones that I have had significant relational struggles with. But it is the working through those difficulties and hurts that binds friendships together. Struggles, when faced with repentance, forge resilience.

The enemy wants us to see failure as final, but God uses it to shape us. This week, when you encounter moments of failure, reframe them as stepping stones to maturity. Keep pressing forward, trusting that God is at work in every struggle, preparing you for greater victories.

Grace be with you; we have much darkness to illuminate.

Further Reading

Philippians 3:13-14

"But one thing I do: forgetting what lies behind...I press on toward the goal for the prize of the upward call of God in Christ Jesus."

Application

This week, interpret struggles or temptations as spiritual training, not setbacks. Learn from them, move forward, and avoid dwelling negatively. When difficulties arise, ask, "How is God using this to strengthen me?" Keep a "growth log" this week: each time you face a struggle, write down the challenge and one lesson or opportunity it presents. For example, "I snapped at my spouse—opportunity to practice patience." At week's end, review your log and pray over each entry, thanking God for His work in you. If you stumble, repent quickly—confess to God or a trusted friend—and take one step forward, like reading a Psalm or serving someone. Pray: "Lord, turn my struggles into steps toward You." Your persistence is a threat to the darkness.

21. Victory Over Temptation

WELCOME TO MONDAY. Our battle against the world, the flesh, and the devil continues.

As we lean into our identity as repentant and forgiven sinners, we must remember how Jesus taught us to pray: "Forgive us our trespasses as we forgive those who trespass against us." Jesus even told a parable about God revoking forgiveness and severely punishing someone who refused to forgive another (Matthew 18:21–35). Imagine how much Satan enjoys the hypocrisy of people showing up on Sunday to claim forgiveness for themselves and then spending Monday growling at everyone who has wronged them. As the proverb goes, unforgiveness is like drinking poison and hoping the other person dies.

Forgiveness is miserably hard. It's why it's included in the Lord's Prayer—not just a suggestion, but a critical component of spiritual health. Consider Joseph in Genesis 45, who forgave his brothers after they sold him into slavery. Years of pain could have hardened his heart, but Joseph chose forgiveness, weeping as he reconciled with them. His story reminds us that forgiveness isn't about denying hurt—it's about releasing it to God. I once held a grudge against a Christian organization who chose not to hire me for a position. For months, I replayed the situation, letting bitterness fester. It was only when I prayed for their blessing—gritting my teeth through it—that I felt the weight lift. Forgiveness didn't erase the pain, but it freed me to move forward.

The Christian life isn't about perfection, but continual repentance. Satan wants us to wallow in unforgiveness or despair over our failures, but God calls us to lean on His grace. This week, when temptation—whether to hold a grudge or indulge in sin—arises, run to God's strength and forgive as you've been forgiven.

Grace be with you; we have much darkness to illuminate.

Further Reading

Matthew 6:14-15

"For if you forgive other people when they sin against you, your heavenly Father will also forgive you. But if you do not forgive others their sins, your Father will not forgive your sins."

Application

When you stumble, don't stay down—repent and return to God immediately. This week, identify one person you've struggled to forgive, whether for a recent slight or a long-held wound. Each day, pray for their well-being, even if it feels forced at first. If temptation to sin arises, don't linger—flee by turning to prayer, Scripture, or a trusted friend. Keep a simple "forgiveness journal" this week: note one act of forgiveness you've extended (to yourself or others) and one way God's grace has met you. Pray: "Lord, teach me that victory lies in persistent repentance and reliance on You." By week's end, reflect on how this practice has shifted your heart toward freedom.

22. THE DISCIPLINE OF WAITING

WELCOME TO MONDAY. Our battle against the world, the flesh, and the devil continues.

Waiting might be the hardest thing we do in battles. The theme of waiting on God appears frequently in the Bible, yet it's often something we'd prefer to ignore. We live in a culture that views waiting as the worst possible scenario, and we've nearly lost the ability to wait without anxiety. Worse still, in seasons of waiting, we tend to catastrophize, imagining the worst-case scenarios playing out in our minds.

We often see ourselves as the grand heroes of our own stories, believing that nothing will happen unless we charge forward. But the truth is, we are minor characters in the grand narrative God is weaving together. Does our part matter? Absolutely. But sometimes, the Field Marshal says wait, and we better be ready to follow that command and prepare for what's next.

The waiting season is not wasted time. God is working, and we must be ready to respond when the time comes.

Grace be with you; we have much darkness to illuminate.

Further Reading

Lamentations 3:25-26

"The Lord is good to those who wait for him, to the soul who seeks him. It is good that one should wait quietly for the salvation of the Lord."

Application

This week, when you find yourself waiting—at a stoplight, in a line, or for an answer—resist the urge to reach for your phone. Instead, train yourself to wait well. Use those ordinary, boring moments to rest in God's presence and trust His timing. Let waiting become a reminder that God is at work, even when you can't see it. *"Lord, help me embrace waiting as a time to be present with You, rather than a distraction to escape."*

23. There Is No Try

Welcome to Monday. Our battle against the world, the flesh, and the devil continues.

"Resist the devil, and he will flee from you." It's a powerful truth to cling to, yet our internal response is often something like, "Okay, I'll try." The problem is, trying doesn't count for nearly as much as we think it does. We tend to judge ourselves by our intentions while judging everyone else by their actions. But if we constantly try and constantly fail, we don't end up any further ahead.

The famous words of Yoda ring true here: "Do or do not. There is no try." Setting out to merely "try" is not the same as setting out to win. Victory over temptation doesn't come from effort alone but from intention backed by the power of God. When we aim for victory, we set a direction of upward momentum and growth, empowered by the Spirit who raised Christ from the dead.

This week, check your intentions. Are you just "trying your best" in the battles you face, or are you setting out to win, empowered by God?

Grace be with you; we have much darkness to illuminate.

Further Reading

James 4:7-8

"Submit yourselves therefore to God. Resist the devil, and he will flee from you. Draw near to God, and he will draw near to you."

Application

Temptation isn't a sign of failure—it's a battlefield where victory is possible. This week, when you feel its pull, don't fight alone. Immediately turn to prayer, scripture, or a trusted friend. Instead of lingering, flee. Instead of relying on willpower, rely on God's strength. *"Lord, when temptation comes, help me run to You and not to sin."*

24. Worry: The Negative Prayer

WELCOME TO MONDAY. Our battle against the world, the flesh, and the devil continues.

A worry is a negative prayer—a foreign-sounding proverb to be sure. But consider this: when we are trapped in worry, our enemies celebrate. Worry consumes our mental energy, distracting us both from prayer and from engaging in the actions we ought to be doing. We become stuck, ruminating over things we cannot control, instead of turning them over to God.

Jesus gave us clear instructions: *Do not worry*. Yet, we've often bought into the lie of self-sufficiency, pushing forward as if we can handle everything on our own. This lie not only wastes our energy but keeps us distant from God. How much time do we spend fretting over things we can't do anything about?

Instead of letting worry paralyze you this week, use it as a trigger to pray. Every time worry creeps in, turn it into a moment of connection with God, presenting your concerns to Him, trusting that He is more than capable of handling them.

Grace be with you; we have much darkness to illuminate.

Further Reading

Philippians 4:6-7

"Do not be anxious about anything, but in every situation, by prayer and petition, with thanksgiving, present your requests to God. And the peace of God, which transcends all understanding, will guard your hearts and your minds in Christ Jesus."

Application

Worry drains energy that could be spent in prayer and action. This week, when anxious thoughts creep in, don't let them spiral—turn them into prayers instead. Each time you catch yourself worrying—STOP IT!—pause and ask: *Have I prayed about this?* Hand it over to God and trust Him with the outcome. *"Lord, help me replace worry with trust, knowing you are in control."*

25. Watch Where You're Looking

Welcome to Monday. Our battle against the world, the flesh, and the devil continues.

When I was learning to ride a motorbike, my dad taught me something that's stuck with me ever since: *"If you stare at that pothole, you will hit that pothole."* The same principle holds true in our spiritual lives. When we fixate on our flaws, failures, and shortcomings, we are bound to repeat them, just like hitting that pothole again and again.

Much of our subconscious programming reinforces these negative patterns. Messages we absorbed from our family of origin or negative experiences growing up have a sneaky way of hijacking our reactions in everyday situations. Our enemies—whether internal or external—would love nothing more than to keep us stuck, staring at those potholes, paralyzed by fear, doubt, or shame.

But here's the truth: God is not fixated on your potholes. He is watching over you and excited about the good works He has prepared for you to walk in. The Creator of the Universe is excited about you. Let that reality sink deep into your soul this week. Lift your eyes from the potholes and focus on the path that God is leading you down—there is much to look forward to.

Grace be with you; we have much darkness to illuminate.

Further Reading

Isaiah 41:10

"So do not fear, for I am with you; do not be dismayed, for I am your God. I will strengthen you and help you; I will uphold you with my righteous right hand."

Application

Where you focus is where you'll end up. This week, when you catch yourself fixating on fears, failures, or distractions, pause and ask: *Am I staring at the pothole, or am I looking toward Christ?* Shift your focus to what is true, good, and eternal. *"Lord, help me fix my eyes on You, not the obstacles in my path."*

26. Headache of the Soul

Welcome to Monday. Our battle against the world, the flesh, and the devil continues.

We've all learned as kids that too much junk food leads to a tummy ache. But what about junk food for the mind? If we consume too much garbage content, we end up with something just as damaging—a "brain-ache" or even spiritual indigestion. Fun fact: I don't go on TikTok because every time I do I lose 45 minutes and then my soul hurts. Many people consume so much mental junk that they operate with a constant fog, unable to focus on the things that truly matter.

It's easy to fixate on sports scores or breaking news, but dwelling on the mysteries of God's kingdom requires effort and intentionality. Remember, our enemy knows the algorithm; he has been breaking the programming of humans for generations. By keeping us distracted and shortening our attention spans, he makes us far easier to manipulate.

It's been said that "the eyes are the window to the soul." What we focus on shapes who we become. This week, guard what you consume. Are your eyes fixed on things that fill you with light, or are you allowing a shadow to creep in? Let's be intentional about what we take in, knowing it impacts the health of our minds, hearts, and souls.

Grace be with you; we have much darkness to illuminate.

Further Reading

Matthew 6:22-23

"The eye is the lamp of the body. So, if your eye is healthy, your whole body will be full of light, but if your eye is bad, your whole body will be full of darkness. If then the light in you is darkness, how great is the darkness!"

Application

This week, try a simple content audit. Track the time you spend on social media, news, TV, or other distractions. At the end of the day, ask yourself: "Did this content feed my soul or drain it?" Then, choose one area to replace with something life-giving—read a passage of Scripture, listen to worship music, or spend a few minutes in prayer. Redirect your focus to things that fill your mind and spirit with light.

27. Guard Your Emotional Energy

Welcome to Monday. Our battle against the world, the flesh, and the devil continues.

This week, you're going to need to guard your emotional energy. We only have so much of it, and I confess I have a nasty habit of wasting it on things that matter zero percent in the face of eternity. It's easy to get sucked into nasty Facebook fights, let a sports team's loss ruin your day, or become outraged over awful customer service. Then, by the end of the day, we wonder why we're exhausted. The world is designed to keep you outraged, anxious, and indignant, draining your emotional reserves. When that's your emotional diet, it's hard to hear the still, small voice of the Father.

Honestly, working in politics, I relearn this lesson often. It's easy to be glued to news cycles, reacting to every headline. I watch my heart grow heavy, my patience thin, and my prayers shallow. I need to reflect on Philippians 4:8 to snap me out of it, urging me to focus on what is true, noble, and praiseworthy. I've started limiting my media intake and replacing it with worship music or silence. Slowly, my soul finds space to breathe again. The enemy thrives when we're emotionally depleted, but God restores us when we steward our energy wisely.

Our emotional energy is a finite resource, like water in a canteen. The world, the flesh, and the devil want to poke holes in it, leaving us parched for the battles that matter—like loving our families or serving our communities. This week, make it a priority to find space each day to quiet your soul and turn off the noise the world wants to feed you. Protect your heart, and let God's peace refill what's been drained.

Grace be with you; we have much darkness to illuminate.

Further Reading

Philippians 4:8

"Finally, brothers, whatever is true, whatever is honourable, whatever is just, whatever is pure, whatever is lovely, whatever is commendable, if there is any excellence, if there is anything worthy of praise, think about these things."

Application

Make a point to end each day with a gratitude practice. Write out three specific things that you are thankful for that happened that day. The pull of the world is to focus on the negative but our soul is refreshed through gratitude.

28. The Grand Distractions

Welcome to Monday. Our battle against the world, the flesh, and the devil continues.

Everyone you meet this week is plowing through their own spiritual desert. The world is set up to ensure they stay there. Vast amounts of our resources are spent trying to escape the drudgery and pain of everyday life. Huge industries of entertainment and sports serve as grand distractions, diverting our attention from confronting and enjoying ultimate reality. Social media, streaming services, and 24/7 news cycles keep us numb, scrolling past the deeper questions of purpose and faith. The enemy delights in this, knowing a distracted heart is less likely to seek God.

Isaiah 55:1–3 calls to us: "Come, all you who are thirsty, come to the waters... Why do you spend your money on what is not bread, and your labor on what does not satisfy?" Contrast this with our culture meme of binge-watching a whole season of a TV series. Hours melted away, but that's about it. Yet the world wants us to believe it's normal to just distract ourselves into oblivion and wonder why we are still thirsty. Jesus's invitation in John 7:37–38—to drink from Him and let rivers of living water flow—reminds us that true satisfaction comes from God, not the world's fleeting distractions.

This week, pause before reaching for the next distraction. Ask yourself if it's numbing you or drawing you closer to God. Choose to invest your time in what nourishes your soul, trusting that God offers something far greater than the world's empty promises.

Grace be with you; we have much darkness to illuminate.

Further Reading

John 7:37-38

"On the last day of the feast, the great day, Jesus stood up and cried out, 'If anyone thirsts, let him come to me and drink. Whoever believes in me, as the Scripture has said, "Out of his heart will flow rivers of living water."'"

Application

Make a point to end each day with a gratitude practice. Write out three specific things you're thankful for that happened that day. The pull of the world is to focus on the negative, but your soul is refreshed through gratitude. Additionally, set a daily "energy check" alarm for midday. When it goes off, ask: "What's draining me right now?" If it's something trivial (e.g., a social media spat), step away and refocus—read a Psalm, take a walk, or pray. If it's a legitimate concern, lift it to God intentionally. By week's end, reflect on how guarding your emotional energy has created space for God's voice. Pray: "Lord, help me steward my emotions to hear You clearly."

29. Thank God for the Struggle

Welcome to Monday. Our battle against the world, the flesh, and the devil continues.

I've been reflecting on some of the sayings of the Desert Fathers, a group of 4th and 5th- century monks who believed the church had become too institutionalized. They lived in the desert to seek God and do battle with the devil. One quote that struck me this week is, "A life of ease drives out the fear of the Lord." This is in stark contrast to our modern sensibilities, which suggest that a good life is a pursuit of ease, comfort, and security.

Fighting temptation is good for the soul—even if you don't defeat the temptation, the mere act of fighting it is itself good for you. The Desert Fathers even taught their disciples to thank God for their temptations because it gave them the opportunity to struggle and ultimately grow. So today, spend a few minutes thinking of the temptation you find the most challenging and thank the Lord for the opportunity to struggle through it. It's a chance to grow into who God is forming you to be.

Grace be with you; we have much darkness to illuminate.

Further Reading

James 1:2-4

"Count it all joy, my brothers, when you meet trials of various kinds, for you know that the testing of your faith produces steadfastness. And let steadfastness have its full effect, that you may be perfect and complete, lacking in nothing."

Application

This week, when you face temptation or hardship, instead of resenting it, thank God for the opportunity to grow. *"Lord, use this struggle to shape me into who You've called me to be."* Rather than asking for an easier path, ask for the strength to walk the one before you with faith and perseverance.

30. Watch for Vulnerability

Welcome to Monday. Our battle against the world, the flesh, and the devil continues.

In every good action movie, there's always that scene where the hero predicts how the bad guy will act. "The villain will be set up over there with a sniper rifle... because that's what I would do if I were him." Now take a minute and think: if you were in charge of making yourself mess up this week, how would you do it? Really think about it. Where are you going to be most vulnerable this week?

If I were in charge of my own destruction this week, I'd make sure I spent too much time absorbing all the pitiful whining and complaining on social media. That would drag me down, starting to internalize a mentality of defeat and powerlessness. But now that I've recognized it, I'm watching out for it.

Where will you be walking without cover this week? Be vigilant in identifying your weak spots and take proactive steps to guard your heart.

Grace be with you; we have much darkness to illuminate.

Further Reading

1 Peter 5:8-9

"Be sober-minded; be watchful. Your adversary the devil prowls around like a roaring lion, seeking someone to devour. Resist him, firm in your faith, knowing that the same kinds of suffering are being experienced by your brotherhood throughout the world."

Application

Identify your most vulnerable moments this week—when you're likely to fall into distraction, discouragement, or temptation. Make a plan now for how you will stay guarded when those moments come.

31. The Long Battle

WELCOME TO MONDAY. Our battle against the world, the flesh, and the devil continues.

It's hard not to get lulled into a sense of complacency in our spiritual lives. We love being inspired by stories of spiritual juggernauts who made huge impacts on the world—people who led revivals, performed miracles, or transformed entire cities. But then we wake up to the challenges of the mundane: the endless emails, grocery store runs, managing family squabbles, and trying to stay focused at work. In the midst of these daily tasks, the lie creeps in that deep, abiding spiritual life is really just for special people.

But growth is always incremental—it's always a little bit at a time, over a long time. People don't wake up as spiritual juggernauts. We only see the highlight reel, not the many years of a long obedience in the same direction. Everything is attainable with a 20-year time horizon. But you have to battle today and tomorrow and next week. As C.S. Lewis is often quoted as saying, "My hope is that when I die, all of hell rejoices that I am out of the fight." Sounds like a good goal.

Grace be with you; we have much darkness to illuminate.

Further Reading

Galatians 6:9

"And let us not grow weary of doing good, for in due season we will reap, if we do not give up."

Application

Spiritual growth isn't about quick wins—it's about faithfulness over time. This week, when you feel weary, remind yourself that small, daily acts of obedience add up. Stay in the fight by committing to one simple spiritual habit—prayer, scripture, or worship—every single day. *"Lord, give me endurance to keep going, knowing that perseverance shapes me for eternity."*

32. Anger

WELCOME TO MONDAY. Our battle against the world, the flesh, and the devil continues.

Anger. It's a bubbling undertone in society—a symptom of the tired despair that comes from the unfulfilled promises of modern life. The more we feel let down by the systems around us, the more anger builds, and as another summer fades, this will become more evident.

Today, you have a choice in how to respond to anger. At some point this week, anger will brush up against you, and you'll be forced to make a decision: will you counterpunch, brood, and pass that hurt onto someone else, or will you remember that "a kind word turns away wrath"? The latter choice isn't easy. It requires supernatural power to pull off a response of grace when everything inside you wants to escalate the situation.

Scripture offers clarity on this emotion. Ephesians 4:26 instructs, "Be angry and do not sin." Anger itself isn't the enemy—it's a signal, often of injustice or hurt. But unchecked, it becomes a tool the devil wields to sow division. I learned this during a late-night pastoral counseling session in Red Deer. A frustrated parishioner's words sparked my own anger, compounded by hunger and exhaustion. Then I remembered HALT—a tool often used in Alcoholics Anonymous to check emotions: Hungry, Angry, Lonely, Tired. This is when we're most vulnerable to the devil's schemes and we're likely to make poor choices. I paused, ate a snack, prayed, and listened with renewed calm, diffusing the tension.

Jesus shows us how to be angry without sin. In John 2:13–17, His righteous anger at the temple's misuse drove Him to act, not destroy. Like Jesus, we can use tools like HALT to direct anger toward God's purposes. If anger dominates your life—if you're constantly hungry, angry, lonely, or tired—it's time to examine deeper patterns. Chronic HALT emotions signal a need to reassess priorities, seek community, or surrender burdens to God. This week, let anger be a prompt to pause, not pounce. Rely on the Spirit to guide your response, turning potential destruction into moments of grace.

Grace be with you; we have much darkness to illuminate.

Further Reading

Proverbs 15:1

"A soft answer turns away wrath, but a harsh word stirs up anger."

Application

Anger is a crossroads—it can either lead to destruction or be surrendered to God. This week, when frustration rises, pause and ask: Is this anger leading me toward righteousness or sin? Instead of reacting, take a breath, pray, and choose a response that reflects Christ. "Lord, help me channel my anger toward what is just and surrender what is not." Use HALT: check if you're Hungry, Angry, Lonely, or Tired. Address those needs—eat, rest, connect, pray—before responding. Journal daily: note one anger trigger and how you applied HALT. If HALT emotions feel constant, reflect: What in my life needs God's realignment? Seek a mentor or friend to discuss. By week's end, see how surrendering anger to God transforms your heart and relationships.

33. Lust

WELCOME TO MONDAY. Our battle against the world, the flesh, and the devil continues.

Lust. We live in an age where people often define themselves by their sexual preferences, expecting the world to not only accept but also celebrate their desires. It's as though our base urges have become the defining feature of human identity. But your desires don't define you—no more than your worst moment defines you. You are a child of the King, specifically called to drive back the darkness around you. You are part of God's plan to establish His kingdom of light wherever you go.

The world normalizes and incentives lust, plastering it across screens and billboards, whispering that indulgence is freedom. The flesh craves instant gratification, and the devil uses these desires to distract us, knowing a heart chasing fleeting pleasures can't seek God. I've felt this pull myself—but these desires are a sure path to slavery and spiritual ruin. It wasn't until I named these desires before God that I found freedom. The story of David and Bathsheba (2 Samuel 11) shows lust's danger—David's fleeting desire led to adultery, murder, and ruin. Yet his repentance in Psalm 51 points to God's mercy, offering a path back to holiness.

Lust thrives in secrecy, but it loses power when exposed to Christ's light. This week, pay careful attention to any dark desires that well up inside you. Shine the light of Christ on them through prayer or accountability. When temptation arises, don't entertain it—redirect it to God's truth. You're not defined by your urges but by your identity as a child of the King. Live out your calling to be a beacon of holiness, trusting God's grace to guide you.

Grace be with you; we have much darkness to illuminate.

Further Reading

1 Peter 2:9

"But you are a chosen race, a royal priesthood, a holy nation, a people for his own possession, that you may proclaim the excellencies of him who called you out of darkness into his marvellous light."

Application

Lust thrives in secrecy, but it loses power in the light. This week, when temptation arises, don't entertain it—redirect it. Instead of feeding the desire, turn to prayer, scripture, or a meaningful task. Fix your eyes on Christ, not fleeting desires. Try a "gratitude reset": when lustful thoughts surface, pause and list three things you're thankful for, focusing on God's provision. Share your struggle with a trusted friend for accountability—confession breaks lust's hold. Each evening, journal one moment you resisted temptation and how God met you. Pray: "Lord, purify my heart and help me desire what is holy." By week's end, reflect on how these steps strengthened your resolve to live as a beacon of God's light.

34. SLOTH

WELCOME TO MONDAY. Our battle against the world, the flesh, and the devil continues.

Sloth. I know you all work hard, but we must stay mindful of the true goal of our efforts. Our goal isn't the dream of retiring with a BMW by the beach. That ideal promises comfort and ease as the ultimate reward for our work, but the truth is, the goalposts will keep moving as you get closer. It's an empty chase.

Instead, we are going to need righteous imagination to solve the problems in this world. As we watch injustice and poverty creep ever more into the world around us, we need to rise up and meet these challenges in our own capacity. Don't let the overwhelming scale of the problems make you cower or slide into inaction. The more we operate at capacity, the more our capacity increases.

Spiritual laziness—the temptation to ignore or retreat from what's difficult—is the real battle. But this week, resist it. Lean into the struggle, and trust that with each step of engagement, God is growing your strength.

Grace be with you; we have much darkness to illuminate.

Further Reading

Proverbs 24:30-34

"I passed by the field of a sluggard, by the vineyard of a man lacking sense, and behold, it was all overgrown with thorns; the ground was covered with nettles, and its stone wall was broken down. Then I saw and considered it; I looked and received instruction. A little sleep, a little slumber, a little folding of the hands to rest, and poverty will come upon you like a robber, and want like an armed man."

Application

Sloth isn't just laziness—it's the failure to engage in what truly matters. This week, when you feel the pull toward passivity or distraction, choose action. Push back by doing the next right thing, no matter how small. Ask yourself: *Am I avoiding something God is calling me to? "Lord, give me the discipline to reject complacency and step into the work You have for me."*

35. Envy

WELCOME TO MONDAY. Our battle against the world, the flesh, and the devil continues.

Envy. It's subtle, but ambition often tempts us to disparage those who appear to have more power, influence, or success than we do. We easily slip into jealousy, especially toward those who seem to be further ahead—perhaps even when they're "doing it wrong." The world has normalized backbiting against the boss, questioning the motives of those in leadership, and cursing political leaders as if it were harmless.

The biblical response to envy presents a paradox. On one hand, Scripture contains the lament of accusing God of allowing the wicked to prosper. But it also offers the challenge that if we are faithful with little, we will be entrusted with more. It's a call to be content and steadfast, resisting the pull to compare and to focus instead on what God has called us to today.

This week, don't get trapped in the lie of comparison. Trust God with your portion, and stay faithful.

Grace be with you; we have much darkness to illuminate.

Further Reading

James 3:14-16

"But if you have bitter jealousy and selfish ambition in your hearts, do not boast and be false to the truth. This is not the wisdom that comes down from above, but is earthly, unspiritual, demonic. For where jealousy and selfish ambition exist, there will be disorder and every vile practice."

Application

Envy poisons gratitude and keeps us focused on what we lack instead of what God has given. This week, when jealousy creeps in, counter it with thankfulness. Any time you feel envy rising, stop and name three blessings in your own life. *"Lord, help me celebrate the good in others and trust that You have given me exactly what I need."*

36. Gluttony

WELCOME TO MONDAY. Our battle against the world, the flesh, and the devil continues.

Gluttony. We live in a world that glorifies overconsumption. From staying on social media apps longer to buying more products, much of the messaging around us is designed to fuel this endless cycle of longing and indulgence. We are constantly bombarded with the expectation to eat, drink, consume, and then do it all over again.

We feast on holidays rather than fast on holy days. But in a culture that invented the buffet, we seem to have lost our appetite for fasting, reflection, and repentance. Have we become so dependent on our phones and instant gratification that we can't even sit in silence, just in case we miss that dopamine ding from our pockets?

In ancient times, fast-days included moments of deep reflection and repentance. Perhaps we could use more of both in our lives today—times to pause, reflect, and reset our spiritual appetite toward God's sustenance rather than the world's.

Grace be with you; we have much darkness to illuminate.

Further Reading

Proverbs 23:20-21

"Be not among drunkards or among gluttonous eaters of meat, for the drunkard and the glutton will come to poverty, and slumber will clothe them with rags."

Application

Gluttony isn't just about food—it's about excess in anything that dulls our hunger for God. This week, when you feel the urge to over-consume, pause and ask: *Is this filling me or numbing me?* Practice self-control by fasting from food or abstaining from media or another indulgence—and use that space to seek God instead. *"Lord, teach me to be satisfied in You rather than in excess."*

37. Greed

Welcome to Monday. Our battle against the world, the flesh, and the devil continues.

Greed. It's a sin that seems to animate entire economies. It's easy to spot greed in others—especially billionaires or corporations—while ignoring the ways it quietly slips into our own lives. We're quick to point fingers at those with obvious excess but much slower to look under the hood of our own spending habits.

The truth is, generosity is at the heart of the gospel. It's the primary way God interacts with us, giving grace, life, and blessings freely. Yet, we often grip tightly to whatever we've been given, shouting, "Mine!" like children clutching their toys. This week, remember that God calls us to open our hands.

You will be given a real opportunity to be generous this week. Don't blink, or you might miss it. Choose generosity—after all, that's the very nature of God's interaction with us.

Grace be with you; we have much darkness to illuminate.

Further Reading

2 Corinthians 9:6-7

"The point is this: whoever sows sparingly will also reap sparingly, and whoever sows bountifully will also reap bountifully. Each one must give as he has decided in his heart, not reluctantly or under compulsion, for God loves a cheerful giver."

Application

Greed convinces us that we never have enough, but the gospel calls us to open hands and generous hearts. This week, when you feel the pull to hold tightly to your money, time, or resources, pause and ask: *How can I be generous instead?* Look for one opportunity to give freely, trusting that God is your provider. *"Lord, help me trust in Your provision and find joy in generosity."*

38. Pride

WELCOME TO MONDAY. Our battle against the world, the flesh, and the devil continues.

Pride is a sneaky trap. It doesn't always present itself as arrogance; sometimes, it hides in our comparisons. We only know if we have a good car by comparing it to others: like older or newer models. The same happens with our spiritual lives. Just because others may be further behind on their journey doesn't mean we're safe. Pride whispers that we've "arrived," but this false security can lull us into spiritual stagnation, leaving us vulnerable.

The antidote to pride is humility. I've been reflecting on a haunting quote from St. Moses the Black, a 4th-century monk who sought God in the Egyptian desert. He said: "You fast, but Satan does not eat. You labor fervently, but Satan never sleeps. The only dimension in which you can outperform Satan is by acquiring humility, for Satan has no humility."

St. Moses knew the power of humility firsthand. Once a gang leader and slave, he was transformed by an encounter with Christ and became a revered monk. His life reminds us that humility isn't just about thinking less of ourselves—it's about recognizing how much we still need God's grace. It's the only weapon that Satan cannot match and the key to defeating pride.

Humility frees us from the trap of self-comparison and opens us to God's work in our lives. This is the way of God's upside-down kingdom.

Grace be with you; we have much darkness to illuminate.

Further Reading

James 4:6

"But he gives more grace. Therefore it says, 'God opposes the proud but gives grace to the humble.'"

Application

Pay attention this week to moments when pride creeps in, especially through comparisons. Instead of dwelling on others, take a moment to thank God for what He's doing in your life. Humility grows when we recognize our dependence on God's grace. Choose one area where you can practice humility, whether by listening more, serving someone quietly, or refraining from judgment.

39. Standing on Guard

Welcome to Monday. Our battle against the world, the flesh, and the devil continues.

There's a line in *O Canada* that we sing proudly but rarely reflect on: "We stand on guard for thee." The "thee" refers to Canada, calling us to vigilance over our nation. But what exactly are we guarding against? It's too easy to insert whichever group we think is "ruining Canada" this week, but those groups are almost certainly different from what the author had in mind back in 1908.

In light of this, we are called to stand on guard not against people but against the dark forces intent on destroying our country, our families and our neighbourhoods. Today, spend some time in prayer, asking for protection for those within your charge, and for God's guidance as we stand on guard.

"Help us to find, O God, in Thee / A lasting, rich reward, / As waiting for the Better Day, / We ever stand on guard."

Grace be with you; we have much darkness to illuminate.

Further Reading

Psalm 72:8

"May he have dominion from sea to sea, and from the River to the ends of the earth!"

Application

This week, be intentional about standing guard over your heart, your home, and your community. When you feel spiritually passive, remind yourself that *you are a watchman*. Each day, take a moment to pray for protection over your family, your church, and your city. Ask: *Where is the enemy trying to creep in, and how can I stand firm?* "*Lord, help me stay vigilant and stand on guard for what truly matters.*"

40. Stay With The Herd

Welcome to Monday. Our battle against the world, the flesh, and the devil continues.

The Bible says the devil prowls around like a roaring lion looking for someone to devour. That often brings up an image of a huge, ferocious lion we'd be powerless against—something we should tip-toe around. But a better image might be Scar from *The Lion King*. He's a mangy, beat-up, old lion—still dangerous, but in a much different way. I remember the hyenas from *The Lion King* plotting to "pick off one of the little sick ones" during the wildebeest stampede. That's a good picture of the devil's strategy—picking us off when we're alone, weak, or sick, while the world is in chaos.

While the devil prowls like a lion, seeking to isolate and attack, the world sells us a story of the lone wolf, the solitary hero—with no one to cover his back. This week, remember that most people you meet are wandering in a spiritual desert, and we've been assured that it's normal. We idealize the image of a man living alone in his cabin in the woods, surviving off the land, but this isn't a reality for most of us.

Humans are designed to live in community and more specifically, in brotherhood. This is nearly the opposite of isolation in the woods. But too often, we settle for shallow connections—maybe a few texts or scrolling X to see what strangers think about the news. This week, create space to spend time with people who challenge you and genuinely want the best for you.

Grace be with you; we have much darkness to illuminate.

Further Reading

1 Peter 5:8-9

"Be sober-minded; be watchful. Your adversary the devil prowls around like a roaring lion, seeking someone to devour. Resist him, firm in your faith, knowing that the same kinds of suffering are being experienced by your brotherhood throughout the world."

Application

Be intentional about strengthening your connections this week. Call or meet up with someone who challenges and supports you. At the same time, reach out to someone who might be feeling alone—help them stay with the herd. Don't get separated from your herd, and do a brother a favour by ensuring no one else is wandering off into that shadowy place.

41. Onward Christian Soldiers

WELCOME TO MONDAY. Our battle against the world, the flesh, and the devil continues.

There is an old hymn that has largely fallen out of use called "Onward, Christian Soldiers." Its language feels nearly foreign to our modern Christian vernacular—the church moving as a mighty army and the foundations of hell quivering at shouts of praise! Yet, on a bleak, dark Monday morning, that sentiment can feel distant and far removed.

This week, you will face challenges amidst the everyday grind. The forces of darkness are rarely so obvious as to make an army seem like the best response. Instead, be on guard for the subtle slipping of your mind, for the nearly unconscious willingness to take the easy way out. God is still on the move—guard your heart and stay in the game.

Grace be with you; we have much darkness to illuminate.

Further Reading

Ephesians 6:10-12

"Finally, be strong in the Lord and in the strength of his might. Put on the whole armour of God, that you may be able to stand against the schemes of the devil. For we do not wrestle against flesh and blood, but against the rulers, against the authorities, against the cosmic powers over this present darkness, against the spiritual forces of evil in the heavenly places."

Application

This week, be aware of the subtle battles in your mind and spirit. Identify one area where you're tempted to take the easy way out and instead, stand firm. Fight with prayer, scripture, and perseverance.

42. Ready for Action

WELCOME TO MONDAY. Our battle against the world, the flesh, and the devil continues.

In order to establish the kingdom of heaven, we are going to need to storm the gates of hell with water guns! And you thought this week was going to be ordinary. God is on the move, and now is not the time to settle for just another week in which you go through the motions.

God's upside-down kingdom is breaking into places we don't expect, and the enemy's tactics are often subtle—relying on the monotony of life to lull us into passivity. The gravity of our routines will try to soothe us back into a calm, passive stupor, convincing us that we're too tired, too distracted or too busy to engage. But the truth is, this battle is ongoing, and it requires us to be active participants.

We must be ready for action. Pay attention this week—look for the signs of where God is at work. The kingdom advances in the small, unexpected moments where love, truth, and grace break through. Don't underestimate the significance of the seemingly mundane. You are part of something far greater than you might realize, and this week could be your moment to advance the kingdom in your sphere of influence.

So watch for the signal. Be alert, and be ready.

Grace be with you; we have much darkness to illuminate.

Further Reading

Matthew 11:12

"From the days of John the Baptist until now the kingdom of heaven has suffered violence, and the violent take it by force."

Application

Be on the lookout this week for an opportunity to bring the kingdom of God into your surroundings—whether through kindness, truth, or boldness. When the moment comes, don't hesitate.

43. God's Perfect Placement

Welcome to Monday. Our battle against the world, the flesh, and the devil continues.

This week will be a challenge. At some point, you will be given the option to do something hard, something uncomfortable, something that requires you to take responsibility. Your instincts may betray you, urging you to take the easy way out, to avoid the discomfort or risk. The world around you will encourage this avoidance, convincing you that it's someone else's problem, not yours.

But remember this: God has placed you exactly where you are for a reason. It's not by accident that you live on your street, work at your job, or interact with the people in your life. Every situation you find yourself in this week is an opportunity—an opportunity to bring God's presence into that space and expand His kingdom.

God doesn't just place us in comfortable or convenient situations. He often places us in difficult ones because He knows that we are needed there. It's easy to think we are powerless or too insignificant to make a difference, but the truth is, even the smallest act of obedience can shine a light into the darkness. This week, when the moment comes to act, don't blink or hesitate—step boldly into it, knowing that God has prepared you for this moment.

Remember, your presence in every situation isn't random; it's a divine assignment.

Grace be with you; we have much darkness to illuminate.

Further Reading

1 Peter 2:9

"But you are a chosen race, a royal priesthood, a holy nation, a people for his own possession, that you may proclaim the excellencies of him who called you out of darkness into his marvelous light."

Application

You are exactly where God wants you to be for a reason. This week, when you feel frustrated by your circumstances, pause and ask: *How can I be faithful right here, right now?* Instead of wishing for a different situation, look for ways to reflect God's light where you are. *"Lord, help me trust that You have placed me here for a purpose."*

44. Overwhelmed by the Scale

Welcome to Monday. Our battle against the world, the flesh, and the devil continues.

There are days when the scale of the problems in the world can feel overwhelming. Loneliness, addiction, broken families, and poverty often seem like insurmountable challenges looming over our society. It's easy to feel powerless in the face of such enormous issues, and that sense of inability is a key part of the enemy's strategy—keeping God's people wide-eyed on the sidelines, frozen in fear or discouragement.

But remember, the belief that there's no hope and nothing you can do becomes a self-fulfilling prophecy. In truth, you are called to make a difference, even if the impact seems small. All problems—no matter how vast—are solved one step at a time. What can you do today to push back against the darkness? Even the smallest act of love, service, or generosity can shine light in the darkest places.

When you find yourself overwhelmed by the scale of the world's problems, pause. Take a breath. Then ask God, "What's the next simple thing I can do?" Find that next step and do it without delay. In God's kingdom, every small step matters, and together, they add up to monumental change.

Grace be with you; we have much darkness to illuminate.

Further Reading

Galatians 6:9

"And let us not grow weary of doing good, for in due season we will reap, if we do not give up."

Application

It's easy to feel powerless in the face of so much brokenness, but God has never called you to fix everything—only to be faithful. This week, when the weight of the world feels too heavy, pause and ask: *Am I looking at this through an earthly lens or an eternal one?* Small acts of faithfulness matter in the kingdom of God. *"Lord, when I feel overwhelmed, remind me that You are at work, and my part—though small—has eternal significance."*

45. Fighting the Darkness

WELCOME TO MONDAY. Our battle against the world, the flesh, and the devil continues.

Pain is real. Sometimes, it's the most real thing when it intensifies. Suffering happens, evil exists, and Jesus experienced this in its fullest darkness. But this isn't a battle of equals, like yin and yang. This is a battle between darkness and light, and Jesus is the victorious King. Remember, when light enters a room, the darkness doesn't stand a chance—darkness is instantly dispelled by the light.

Yet sometimes we get fixated on the "why" of evil instead of focusing on our ability to do something about it. We act as if Jesus isn't getting ready to return on His white horse, leading an army of light to vanquish the darkness. The truth is, we've been specifically placed here to help deal with the evil and suffering around us.

So ask yourself: What are you going to do about it this week? How are you going to make things better? If you don't have an answer yet, take some time to find one. We need more lights on in our fight against the darkness.

Grace be with you; we have much darkness to illuminate.

Further Reading

John 1:5

"The light shines in the darkness, and the darkness has not overcome it."

Application

Darkness doesn't retreat on its own—it must be pushed back. This week, when you encounter despair, injustice, or spiritual attack, respond with light. Instead of complaining about the darkness, bring the presence of Christ into it. Speak truth, show kindness, and pray boldly. *"Lord, make me a light that shines in the darkness, no matter how small it may seem."*

46. Living to Fight Another Day

Welcome to Monday. Our battle against the world, the flesh, and the devil continues.

I hate to be the one to tell you, but something will go wrong this week. The world has a way of breaking down and throwing our plans off course. We get a cold, a flat tire, or an email that derails our entire week. When life throws these curveballs, it's often difficult to know how to respond. Everyone has a friend who embodies Eeyore from *Winnie the Pooh*, who can gloomily respond to everything, "The sky has finally fallen. Always knew it would." This naturally pulls the energy out of the room. Then there's the over-the-top optimist, eager to spin every hardship as the best thing that ever happened—a little too much like a budget Tony Robbins.

We can't control the bumps in the road, but we can control how we respond. Our enemies want nothing more than to drive us to despair, but we are not called to ignore or gloss over real, present challenges. The truth is, life is hard, and it's okay to have off days. Some days are so difficult that they become 'try again tomorrow' days. But that's the key—we live to fight another day. Struggles are critical moments for growth; challenges make us stronger.

Lamentations 3:22-23 reminds us, "The steadfast love of the Lord never ceases; his mercies never come to an end; they are new every morning; great is your faithfulness." You are not defined by one bad day, one failed plan, or one challenge. Instead, you are renewed each morning with mercy and strength to face what lies ahead.

Grace be with you; we have lots of darkness to illuminate.

Further Reading

Lamentations 3:21-26

"But this I call to mind, and therefore I have hope: The steadfast love of the Lord never ceases; his mercies never come to an end; they are new every morning; great is your faithfulness. 'The Lord is my portion,' says my soul, 'therefore I will hope in him.' The Lord is good to those who wait for him, to the soul who seeks him. It is good that one should wait quietly for the salvation of the Lord."

Application

When challenges arise this week, take a moment to pause and reflect. Are you responding with despair, false positivity, or with trust in God's mercy? Instead of letting the struggles of the day overwhelm you, remember that God's mercy and faithfulness renew every morning. If today feels like a loss, pray for the strength to live and fight again tomorrow.

47. Net Worth is not Self Worth

WELCOME TO MONDAY. Our battle against the world, the flesh, and the devil continues.

If you're not careful, you'll miss the lie that your self-worth is determined by your net worth. Have you allowed numbers on a website to define your value? The stock market is a mysterious entity—affecting lives in material ways while being, at its core, an idea. Some cynics call it "a graph of rich people's feelings" or "astrology for men." Certainly, money is made and lost, but the market often functions like a pagan god we work to appease. We scoff at ancient people bowing to a golden calf, yet a bronze bull stands proudly outside the New York Stock Exchange.

This misplaced focus distracts us from the true Provider. Scripture reminds us that the Lord "owns the cattle on a thousand hills" (Psalm 50:10), and Jesus assures us of God's care in Matthew 6:28-30: "Consider the lilies of the field, how they grow: they neither toil nor spin; yet I tell you, even Solomon in all his glory was not arrayed like one of these." If we truly believe God provides everything, do our actions and our transactions validate that belief? Or is this just a Sunday School sentiment that falls apart in the real world?

Allow Jesus' words to haunt you this week: "For where your treasure is, there your heart will be also" (Matthew 6:21).

Grace be with you; we have lots of darkness to illuminate.

Further Reading

Matthew 6:19-21

"Do not lay up for yourselves treasures on earth, where moth and rust destroy and where thieves break in and steal, but lay up for yourselves treasures in heaven, where neither moth nor rust destroys and where thieves do not break in and steal. For where your treasure is, there your heart will be also."

Application

This week, limit how often you check your bank account or the stock market. Trust God's provision instead of fixating on numbers. Watch for an opportunity to be generous—it's the best cure for the grip wealth has on us.

48. Gratitude in Action

Welcome to Monday. Our battle against the world, the flesh, and the devil continues

.We spend a great deal of time categorizing those around us. Often, most of our conversations revolve around who is awful at their job, who isn't as smart as we are, or who doesn't deserve to be in charge. Workplace chatter is filled with this kind of talk, but somehow, we rarely get around to talking about who's doing great.

Complaining often feels like our native language. It's easy to bond over what's wrong with the world, but let's take a step back and recognize how much we have to be thankful for. We live in a time of abundance—things like forced-air furnaces and cars would have been beyond the wildest dreams of many of your ancestors. Yet, we still find things to grumble about. Worse yet, our everyday grumbling is often a subtle critique of God's goodness and provision, and that's a habit worth reversing.

In the midst of a world tilted toward complaining and ranking the flaws of everyone around us, our enemies thrive. Criticism is easy. Genuine praise is much harder.

Grace be with you; we have much darkness to illuminate.

Further Reading

Philippians 4:8

"Finally, brothers and sisters, whatever is true, whatever is noble, whatever is right, whatever is pure, whatever is lovely, whatever is admirable—if anything is excellent or praiseworthy—think about such things."

Application

This week, you have the opportunity to break the cycle, even just for a moment. Find someone who deserves a compliment—more than just a simple "thanks" or "good job"—but a real, heartfelt acknowledgment of the good you've noticed in them. Write them a three-sentence compliment to show them that their efforts have not gone unnoticed. Trust me—this will change their entire week.

49. YES. YOU. CAN

Welcome to Monday. Our battle against the world, the flesh, and the devil continues.

Do you ever wonder if our Father in Heaven just shakes His head at us the same way we sometimes shake our heads at our kids? I remember one time when my four-year-old was struggling to put on pants for no apparent reason. I came to the door to find her lying on the ground, pants around her ankles, moaning, "I can't do it." Naturally, it was time to leave and this wasn't helping. In that moment, it was hard not to seethe and blurt out, "YES. YOU. CAN."

I don't accept this kind of self-sabotage from my kids. We lovingly parent them to learn that they *can* do basic tasks and that they're welcome to ask for help when things get tricky. But I don't let the lie of "I can't do it" take root.

Yet, I watch God's children willfully self-sabotage all the time. We hear testimonies of missionaries or people who have endured great trials, and our first thought is often, "Oh wow, I could never do that." Is our Heavenly Father sitting in Heaven, shaking His head, going, "YES. YOU. CAN"? The Bible is clear: *"I can do all things through Christ who strengthens me"* (Philippians 4:13). For some reason, we apply this verse to sports (which aren't mentioned in the Bible) rather than to God's children learning to do hard things in obedience to Him.

Grace be with you; we have much darkness to illuminate.

Further Reading

Philippians 4:12-13:

"I know how to be brought low, and I know how to abound. In any and every circumstance, I have learned the secret of facing plenty and hunger, abundance and need. I can do all things through Christ who strengthens me."

Application

This week, you will witness or be asked to do something difficult. Your gut instinct might be, "Oh wow, I could never do that." Recognize this thought for the lie it is—a lie designed to keep you from doing all that God is asking you to do. Call it out, and trust God's strength to help you begin. As a reminder, write "YES. YOU. CAN." on a sticky note and place it somewhere prominent. Let it encourage you to start doing the hard things.

50. Amazing Grace

WELCOME TO MONDAY. Our battle against the world, the flesh, and the devil continues.

Let's take a minute this morning to remember where we've been. How many times we've battled and won? There's a line in *Amazing Grace* that goes, "Through many dangers, toils, and snares I have already come." I know this is true in my life, and I am certain it is in yours. As you gear up for the week, reflect on all the struggles that God has brought you through.

As we look ahead to the coming week, know that God will lead you through whatever lies ahead. Expect it. Watch for it. Know that the Lord leads us to good places, not necessarily easy places. Be mindful that Jesus taught us to pray, "Lead us not into temptation, but deliver us from evil." He has delivered us in the past and will do so again.

Grace be with you; we have much darkness to illuminate.

Further Reading

Psalm 23:1-6

"The Lord is my shepherd; I shall not want. He makes me lie down in green pastures. He leads me beside still waters. He restores my soul. He leads me in paths of righteousness for his name's sake. Even though I walk through the valley of the shadow of death, I will fear no evil, for you are with me; your rod and your staff, they comfort me. You prepare a table before me in the presence of my enemies; you anoint my head with oil; my cup overflows. Surely goodness and mercy shall follow me all the days of my life, and I shall dwell in the house of the Lord forever."

Application

Take five minutes today to reflect on where God has brought you from. Write down one or two moments where His grace carried you. Let gratitude shape your outlook this week.

51. Take the Stairs

Welcome to Monday. Our battle against the world, the flesh, and the devil continues.

When I was in university, I made a conscious decision to take the stairs rather than the escalator in the main building. I wasn't overweight, but I figured every bit of exercise and intentionality helps. Even now, I make a point to take the stairs when possible. It's a small thing, but a good thing.

Spiritual life has a similar effect. The world offers countless escalators—paths of least resistance that require no effort but also lead nowhere meaningful. The wide, easy road may feel comfortable, but it doesn't build strength. C.S. Lewis warned about this in *The Screwtape Letters*:

"Indeed, the safest road to Hell is the gradual one—the gentle slope, soft underfoot, without sudden turnings, without milestones, without signposts."

No one drifts into spiritual maturity. You don't grow in faith by accident. Strength is built through effort, discipline, and choosing the harder but better path. When we take the stairs spiritually—prioritizing prayer, Scripture, and intentional discipleship—we develop endurance for the battles ahead.

Jacob once had a vision of a ladder connecting heaven and earth, with angels ascending and descending (Genesis 28:12). It was a powerful image of divine connection, but also of movement—climbing, striving, engaging with God. Spiritual life is like that ladder. It requires effort, a continual upward climb, and the willingness to step into what God is doing. The alternative? Letting the world's escalators carry you slowly down in the wrong direction.

Grace be with you; we have much darkness to illuminate.

Further Reading

Hebrews 12:11

"For the moment all discipline seems painful rather than pleasant, but later it yields the peaceful fruit of righteousness to those who have been trained by it."

Application

This week, every time you find yourself climbing stairs, take a moment to reflect: are you taking the stairs in your spiritual life as well? Are you choosing the harder but better path of prayer, scripture, and spiritual discipline? Small, daily choices shape who you become. Keep climbing.

52. Choose Joy

Welcome to Monday. Our battle against the world, the flesh, and the devil continues.

One of the most meaningful funerals I've ever attended was for a woman in her thirties who was a foster parent. Her story was heartbreaking—cancer, a life cut short, leaving behind a husband and kids who needed her. And yet, at her funeral, everyone was given a picture with two simple but powerful words: Choose Joy.

She chose joy even in the midst of great pain, impending loss, and, ultimately, death. We still have that picture. It's a reminder that joy isn't just something that happens to us—it's something we choose.

Satan hates joy. He hates laughter. He wants our hearts heavy, weighed down by fear, anxiety, and bitterness. Some of the greatest joys in life come from the pure, unfiltered laughter of little kids, but as we grow older, the weight of the world tries to smother that childlike delight. The enemy would love nothing more than for us to believe that joy is reserved for people with easy lives.

But can we rejoice at the goodness of God even when life is unsettled and full of problems? Can joy become a spiritual discipline—something deeper than a fleeting emotion, something beyond just the cognitive exercise of counting our blessings? True joy isn't the same as gratitude. It's not merely listing what's good; it's experiencing a profound, heart-level delight in God, even when life is hard.

This week, make the intentional choice to rejoice—not because life is easy, but because God is good.

Grace be with you; we have much darkness to illuminate.

Further Reading

Habakkuk 3:17-18

"Though the fig tree should not blossom, nor fruit be on the vines, the produce of the olive fail and the fields yield no food, the flock be cut off from the fold and there be no herd in the stalls, yet I will rejoice in the Lord; I will take joy in the God of my salvation."

Application

At some point this week, you will feel the weight of life pressing in. When that moment comes, make a deliberate choice to rejoice. Not just to be thankful, but to step into deep, defiant joy. Laugh freely, praise God wholeheartedly, and refuse to let the enemy steal what God has given you. Choose joy.

ABOUT THE AUTHOR

Chad Krahn is a former church planter, current City Councillor in Red Deer, Alberta, and a devoted husband and father of five children. Passionate about community building and spiritual growth, Chad actively guides others in their spiritual journeys. Holding a Master's degree in Theological Studies from Taylor Seminary, Chad brings deep biblical insight and extensive experience into his work. His experiences in ministry, public service, and as a foster parent have shaped his distinctive perspective on integrating faith into daily life. This devotional project reflects Chad's commitment to encouraging individuals as they navigate the challenges of faith, community, and personal growth.

Writers Wanted

Nine Tries Publishing is looking to partner with writers from across the world in a variety of genres. From children's picture books to biographies, novels and devotionals, we're interested in everything. You don't have to be an established author or have a literary agent to get in touch with us—nor does you project require a large audience. What matters most to us is your passion and your prose (or verse if poetry is your thing). To that end, feel free to connect with us via email at contact@ninetries.co.uk, visit our website at ninetries.co.uk or connect with us on Instagram (ninetries.publishing). For those who are interested, we also offer personalised literary services, which range from coaching and editorial work to help with drafting your entire book. If that interests you, connect with us via email (contact@ninetries.co.uk).

www.ingramcontent.com/pod-product-compliance
Lightning Source LLC
Chambersburg PA
CBHW060500080526
44584CB00015B/1490